AF434491

in loving memory
of all of the loves
of history
buried

OF FEAST AND FAMINE

that I was still good

by Mealla Sweet

Published in 2023 by
Machete by Moonlight
the Bend of the Upper Deschutes, USA

Copyright © 2023 by Mealla Sweet

Cover image Public Domain 2011

ISBN 979-8-218-24174-2 (paperback)

All rights reserved. No part of this work may be reproduced in any form or by any means without written permission and express consent of the copyright owner.

CONTENTS

INTRODUCTION

There came a time in my life where I truly comprehended I was the problem in my life. Everything that came through me as I experienced it did little for me but lead to increasing isolation. As empowering as it was for me to explore parts of life that so fascinated my inquiries and imbued me with life from within and beyond, there came a day where I had to reconcile it was unrelatable for others, how it expressed itself out of me, or they would have related to it in honesty as humans do so so freely amongst each other. Any would have, but eventually none did. Not even my own family. I was so blind that I thought all I was offering outward was more relatable or would be of service somehow. That it just hadn't found its way yet.

Well over a decade later, I see it different. There isn't a soul in my literal life I am close with anymore. There isn't anyone I would trust to be most honest with me. Not after what I've seen. And that's a place that no one but me can help me out of. Though we all have vivid experiences and live wondrous lives, that I know for certain, have always known since as young as I can recount, I was the common element of friction and unrelatability. It was me and my distinct lens towards enchantment and relationality and perceiving unseen openings for healing and being so freely contemplative with it all being more closely connected that led me to being alone. When all I was exploring and expressing outwardly was my own joy and challenges with ecology and watersheds and local food and hand crafted medicines and the earth and eventually tiny little tidbits of loving my ancestral dream world that were cohesively captivating me to move in particular ways. Even in that innocence, any tiny chapter of it, there was something deeply wrong.

Actually, that was probably the root of my undoing. Those entanglements. I looked around and saw so many who world soul embraced freely for those very things. Even those things relating together. Countless individuals in countless ways. It was me whom it did not, and my attempts to delve into the contrasting layers between what was coming through me and the ways in which it was causing me escalating problems did little but further compound my own estrangement. As years upon years passed by, my alienation only exacerbated through my wanting to be enough as I was and as I was becoming, to keep, let alone build, relationships. Yet, one by one, relationships fell out of my life simultaneously, each hand hunted out by others whom I had no relations with because of who I imperfectly was and wasn't all at the same time. Eventually, as frustrations mounted for me, I even chose to let some go, the last few left. I'd seen too much.

Having been bled out and hardened through the process, I didn't think it so personal initially, each individual circumstance being mostly my issue, each step along the way. It wasn't that I was avoiding reflection. I've always been my own worst critic. It's more that I'd heard first hand confessions about the characters and momentum that were working to ensure I was increasingly boxed into isolation. Friends were made to be cautious at best and fearful at times to relate with me openly, according to them, and it wasn't only because of me. There were real humans that were hellbent on me having no support systems remaining, and I was a nobody by all sane measures, so it made no sense. I leaned harder into it at my own demise.

It wasn't until I was all on me own, that I came to see it as simple as such: that I was indeed what didn't add up. Truth be told, the aforementioned entanglements are the days and seeds that opened the doors that got me into the mess that I came to experience as abusive. Experienced as abusive for me maybe only because I didn't agree with having to agree explicitly. My free thinking spirit and heart for loving as I was moved to, not how others dictated to me I must and must not, were ultimately why I was not enough. Because I believed life wasn't meant to be lived in externally defined boxes allying for side making, but there was an untruth in that, wasn't there.

Hindsight, I've been hard humbled to acknowledge it may very well exist as necessary, slightly rigid side making. Afterall, how many identities are built upon such dimensions and the camaraderie they find therein? Not only that, but it has given humans safe spaces to other freely and righteously as they best see fit without considerations or pressure for internalizing reflections much being a thing, so long as one agrees with the rules of the camp of their choosing.

My questioning of those dimensions ultimately came across as more akin to questioning the very foundations of others. And as I chose my self in process, so too did they choose their selfs appropriately. That even my old once friends had each in their own ways conspired to participate in undoing me, at times as though in tandem with each other, alongside what I endured in sum collectively, spoke volumes when my personal reflections and reconciliation factored into the equations. Those that knew me most. But on the flipside, that simply letting go of me, however, going their own way and walking away from me alone was somehow not enough either. That is what I could not fathom. Maybe it was some of them that signed me up for it. Whatever it was I experienced. Who am I to know. It sure felt that way. Looking back, I wonder if that's why they made their way into my life to begin with, but to say that, is to say near too much.

This work is the documentation of all that will be buried upon its completion. Internally and externally, though all for naught was it not. The interiority shelter found through it all was somehow worth all

of it. I saw the web of life eyes wide open and awake,
not simply in dreams preparing me to see it anymore.
I felt into the subtle terrain differences between God
and God's hands, God within and God without, God
and world soul, world soul and humanity, the body and
our bodies, nature and sky, divinity and God, Source
and matter, my own lens into the troubles as to why
humans relate to the earth and one another how they
do. But the wise ones, they don't speak of these things
relationally for good reasons. All of history buried
those that labored to. And I may just be another pearl
collected by the invisible hands along that necklace of
fools collected. More like fools' gold, left for dead.

They are all a part of it. The embodiment and
aliveness of it. The lovers, the fighters, the haters, the
healers, the educators, the makers, dare I even say
those that move between things. None really can't
not be. Each in their own way, all of them playing any
noticing, seemingly, as though none are being honest
wholly. Well, not in a language I could hear in context
of the whole. I came to truly grasp that all that are
wanted, are freely embraced. All that are not, well,
they are more like me. Despite that harshness, I do
know I am far from special in my alienation sensing.

Thus, the real crazy making was me not early
enough recognizing the wholeness of world soul as a
cohesive body in its multitude of movements regardless. And it worked beautifully as it was. I was the

empty vessel that had nothing that calculated out as being of value. Or it would have found its way through the many years of vulnerably putting myself out there. It would have found its way organically and never would've come to be progressionally felt as personally oppositional in so many directions to begin with. I was painstakingly shown that's how it worked for the many whom it did, by a long shot, being organically enfolded within. As they say, all roads lead back to our own self eventually. And so here I am.

Any crumbs felt as of support through the years ultimately proved to be but illusions in my own mind leading me to seeing my self as I was. I am finally being most honest. Maybe I will've buried myself in the end. Maybe it was always me. Maybe that was even what I wanted without the humility to be honest about it. But I am now, and what is seen can't be unseen. A deliverance I would not've wanted, but am grateful for nonetheless. No weight nor care do I need to carry anymore. Thank you to all that were a part of my undoing. Any segment of it. Known but mostly unknown certainly. This work would not've been possible without such a drastic dissolution, synchronicity led no less. So there's that to grapple with.

Having said that, the world needs basic grunt laborers too. Those that toil through all the thankless work. It's what makes the world go round. It wouldn't work if some didn't accept such places in life. That what some perceive as gifts within are but for their own self to witness and resiliently adapt to the world around them, 'tis not lost on me. World soul alone chooses who it wants to lift up, in what ways, and who it does not. The most subtle of nuances sometimes make all the difference depending on who they are coming from. Control being fundamental to its efficacy. Contradictions abound and seem necessary somehow, hindsight, after seeing the unspeakable in what I have seen. I know this wholeheartedly now. What gifts are wanted in what ways, in what times, and brought through by whom, delineated from those that, for lack of better words, are simply not.

After countless years of tears resisting such simple teachings, I know where I belong finally because the world showed me. It proved to me I was always where I belonged in those ways. While it was okay indeed to take up the space that is mine alone in this world, with that responsiblity comes great consequences sometimes far beyond their worth. Though far different too am I now than I once was, already have I paid them dearly, lifetimes beyond anything that has come out of me. Forged now newly by all I've lived through, as we all are. I know 'tis the gift to look out at the world however I am moved to, so long as it is from within that I am listening to. That I do not, did not have to, grant others the permission to take that from me, no matter how strongly they disagreed with or disapproved of me or how I move in my own life.

Belonging was always to choose being home in me and needn't be anything more. That we don't need to be seen to belong at all, by anyone outside of our own self, and by gatekeepers most of all. I am freed to no longer waste energy pretending otherwise. There are countless inspirations in time and across time who found their own way, whether in their time or by way of leaving seeds behind for it to become possible after departing from it. The sum of all aforementioned is a gift that summer solstice will forever forward be my reminder of.

Without further ado, confessions of a villain:

FOOD FOREST

My secret garden
isn't cultivated
how most are
nothing like Eve's
would be
nor Lilith's
truly
I looked
down those pathways
I chose
differently

I am a daughter
of the North
a daughter of the North's
timeless ways
all that has been
still is being
hunted in us
hunted by world soul
no less
hunted in our selves
what we are most
loved and hated
for
but isn't it like that
for all of us

I am as much of nature
as I am
of sky
a soul dancing
between
no mediation
do I need
though teachers
and loved ones
there are many

My garden
like the spirit
that moves
in and through me
moves me
is of a wilder
nature
but as only
my anam cara
could teach me
not entirely wild
either

NOT HUNG UP

The greats were right
that life
life doesn't much care
about goodness
or badness
in most individuals
not really
'tis not so simple

Karma is delivered
at whim
by world soul
in a given moment
the energy must go
somewhere
subtle things
sometimes
therefore
light years more costly
than their true measure
or worth
for all that is
projected
and tacked onto them

Blind spots
of world soul

be damned
like plugging leaks
that were a pipe
more channel like
without realizing
sometimes
'twere also of
the fountains of life

The illusion
of justice
a most laughable
facade
then
once one has seen it
for all that it is
it simply happens
and
it's too costly to care
in many ways
outright dangerous
too

Our present moment
for such things
'tis not that different
than centuries past

millennia's even
only masks and roles
change
don't they

The shapeshifting nature
just as the hero
has a thousand faces
so too does the enemy

TO NULLIFY

I don't really like
the sound of my own voice
isn't that telling
the layered meanings
behind such things
I always wanted it
to sound
more like another's
any not me
not in any way
wanting
what any other had
I love the life
I've lived
am still living in
but more in simply
not wanting
the sound that is mine
feeling ever
an awkward trembling
frozen
in stiffened chords
like an instability

Neck injuries
haunted me
until I began to speak

but speaking out
breaching through
veils of silence
showed me why
their was troubles
to begin with

So much time
and tending
now spent
to release
so many poisons
from drinking from
poisoned wells
that were sold
as medicines
so very long ago

It's a good thing
the medicines
we truly need
already
dwell within
each

WHAT IF

What if sometimes
denying the world
our gifts
in time
is our gift
to world soul
to our self
in it all
to enjoy it
just for us

What if world soul
itself
is not strong enough
in a given grace
or interested
to lovingly hold us

What if our own love
alone
is all that is meant
for us
to carry us through
such moments

Lessons I am so grateful for
yet never would've wanted

DIMINISHING BLOSSOMINGS

Watch any child
submersed right into
life's rich pageant
with trials a plenty
too young
and you will quickly see
we were born
to do alchemy
as though
dancing back and forth
between
darkness and light
with unmediated
grace and ease
empowered
by simply being loved
through it

What if we weren't
meant
to stay in this realm
in only one of them
like seasons
like diurnal pulsing
life
without it
'twould eventually

become
less life
and light filled
wouldn't it

LITTLE GOLDEN WEAVER

How much
of what the world
prejudices Europe for
which is to say
descendants of that land
time immemorially speaking
is really
an aversion within
for how they got that way
wherever it is
they are
or perceive they are
Europeans included
Europeans that disapprove
of Europe
and their interpretations
of its spirit

The entanglements
of what grew
globalization
and upheld
the violent phenomenon
that have always
been its markings
are as vast
and complex

and diverse
as the species
of the earth
nearly
compounding
trillions of interactions
one after another
later
agreements and disagreements
each unable to see
the bigger picture
all shaping it
moving it along
in every moment
our moment
the accumulation
of all of 'em
that've been

Yet like the web of life
one cannot pull
on any string
without finding it
interwoven
with all of the rest
'tis a fool's errand
to think ya can do so

to think any can do so
to think it so simple
and yet it is
then again
isn't it
rather simple
in its wholeness

EIDETIC VISION

When the dust settles
when the air clears
when all that remains
is dust
is raw particles
when fires have ravaged
the whole of your life
down into every molecule
that you are
that you thought you were
that others may've thought
you were too
or what would limit you
or how they may've
wanted it to
or do you let them still

The crucification
you would not've asked for
the terrain
where terror
becomes blessing
discardment the gift
projection the uplifting
where hatred becomes
God loving instead

filtered through your eyes
washed clean

When you feel into that
can you give thanks
in prayer
for it

A DICKINSON CURSE OR WORSE

16   I became
an untouchable
and yet
I could not've
cared less

WESTERN MYTHS PART I

It's a very Wild West
thing
to get away
from it all
from all cities
to want to get away
from everything
the people
the noise
the hustle
the bustle
the rat race
the crazy making
until one realizes
the impossibility
of not being
a part of it
even when
far from it
a run out illusion
in the Americas
isn't it
that damn ocean
so many ran towards
I ran towards
until I ran
up against it

How many
since the beginning
lost everything
for the dream
sold to them
literally
that they could
desperations
vested
all in
recklessly even
the false relief
and then grief
anger and resentments
with no room
to hold room
for much any of it
to learn
that that resistance
'tis what is hunted
about it now
and then too then
wasn't it
hence the selling
of said illusions
far removed
from any honesty

about the conditions
one would land into
that then
had to be
made do with

All one can do
truly
time tested
and proven now
in better and worse ways
if we were wise enough
to learn from all
is choose
how in one's own heart
they go about it

There is no opt out
button
box
and free tickets
they'll come
with an even greater cost
as some have lived it
to show us
even in opting out
there is still dependence

not interdependence
but co-dependence
it's been made
that way
and none should be made
to feel guilty
for having survived it
for having strived
to thrive in it
given what it is
and how little
the world
has truly seen it
for what it is
within globalized
exchange
inflationary pressures
compounded with
global demands too
the latter of which
has never been
homogenous
ever

And sure
we could talk about history
until night gives way

to morning
but that's not living
in it
what of our present
moment
we find ourselves in

Why hate on any
for them having found
ways to thrive
like any not them
know much about
how any got to
where they are
or where they really are
now
for that matter
few know the half
of how they got to
where they are
themselves
or even where they are
either
thus projections
are only all the more
untrue
how resentments

22   and hatred
grow and brew
detaching individuals
further and further
from reality
in all directions
this happens
near equally
doesn't it

NOT BUILT LIKE THEM

Everyone on the planet
is financially abusing
others
in some fashion
not one is immune
not truly
so long as the system
is what it is
none really play it
that different
not from what
I've seen
'tis best
to choose
to live

I've released concern
with those who do so
to me
or would
or to others
anymore
even if I should
have concern
that is

I've no more agency

into what I don't see
and have no control
over anything
literally
nothing
not even that which I do see
anyways
to do much about it

What stresses me more
or would
if I carried on so
is caring about it
worrying about it
if it's happening
how it's happening
if it is
or what to do about it
because even if 'tis
and intentional
it's their prerogative
all of theirs
all that consent to it
rules that make it
as such
rules I've no agency
or influence

upon
my vote
doesn't even matter
so why would it
in larger matters

So reckon do I
all I can do
is be me
and it's what feels best
being me
to honor
how I'm moved to move
even when movement
is in stillness
silence
shadows
dynamism too
is movement
flowing
in any given moment

THE UNATTENDED FUNERAL

They came to bury me
until one day
I let them
I realized
I wanted to let them
that it was okay
that all was right
in letting them
do to me
as they wanted
in those ways
and so I let them bury me
while still breathing
I let them bury me
alive
and I breathed
still
I breathed stillness
into the release
and I saw
how when others bury you
but you live on
still
that that death
that death is more
theirs to grieve
if you let it
be so

THANK YOU X

We like to think
we understand
the works of those
that've come before us
revolutionary thinkers
especially
the frameworks and importance
of their works
but how often
do we miss
what was
most important
about them
and what their life
in its whole
as its own art form
offers to teach us
still
teaches us in our now
from where they were
in time
and what they made
with it
and what became
of them
and where we are
now
how the fabric of things

are misconstrued
too often
in future times

We're not made
to try to remake
their ways
or their dreams
to come to be
even the most inspiring
of gifts
we're made to learn
all they were
to witness
how world soul
responded to them
and why
what was made
out of
by others
the effects
of their works
that there're lessons
in all of it

LITTLE BELLY LAUGH

Next leveling up
with compassion
is learning
in all the ways
how if you weren't you
you might hate you too
and then loving
even those
who hate you
too
made most possible
because you love you

THE FAILING HEALTH CARE INDUSTRY

Untold diaspora
here in America
well,
most anywhere
likely
have living memories
of pasts
pasts we don't much
talk about
families so haunted
by all that led them
to be here
that to talk about it
'tis to bear too much
especially when compounded
especially when
all that 'twas
is not really understood

Yet,
living
living in today's cultural climate
all global like
it's honestly
only intensified
hasn't it
but so too

has the violence
that silence
is violence
what crazy times
we live in
isn't it

European diaspora
likely
speaking from my lens
and all I have witnessed
witness still
are the least understood
and most projected about
in the whole
of the world
in this generation
but I'm not one
keeping count
just observing
as I'm led from beyond
to witness

It's not about
going back
nor paramountcy
for any

just as it's not about
jumping forward
either
but with pressures
all around us
hostile are many
it's about awakening
to who we are
and remembering
that listening
is not about
taking on projections
from any direction
that the healing journeys
for others
for individuals
are not always
honest or reconcilable
with our own truths
that the complexities
of life
do not work like that
and sometimes
sometimes what is assured
is needed
for healing
for better relating

is not at the root
of it
at all
anyways
prevailing
medical systems
alone
and the peoples' buy-in
to them
teach us this

ALL ROADS LEAD BACK TO GLOBALISM

I care not much
for the travails
of America
this land
that has sheltered me
so lovingly
since the beginning
the land that is
knowing the very footsteps
of all of my ancestry
here well before
America's beginning
knowing the hearts
and all they endured
as for us
no mediation
does nature
nor Source
need
for knowing us either

I am grateful
for all it has
gifted the world
most of which
will likely ne'er
be acknowledged
a long list

I've been shown
as attempts to force
the swallowing
of others' takes on it
have all regurgitated
most of which
are disempowering
for all but the few
the hands moving
things
behind the scenes
as my beloved Europe
too knows
all too well
somewhere in that body
since it first too met
globalization
after which
everything changed

More of the same
really
these days
so little
'tis surprising
5,000 miles later
to've resolved
next to nothing

by choice
by force
the world
now made small
all roads led
down the same road
a road I found
I could not walk upon
its making
nor its destruction
fore to walk it
in either direction
would've been
would be
to live another's story
a multitude of others'
that were mostly
untrue to mine
in near all ways
like thinking
late stage Rome
since the fall of Boudicca
served Europe at all

And so the travails
of this place
now mimicking those
of world soul

not unironically
and all it wants
to proliferate
in world making
as of this pencil
striking down on paper
mostly feels
untrue
in near all ways
these days
but the blessings
the complexity that
'tis America
have bestowed upon me
are vastly more many

Time spent
intimately
in Indian Country
time spent
witnessing
black communities
and their outreaching's
alongside a multitude of others
all rubbed off on me
taught me the importance
showed me my shallowness
hindsight, previously

the shuddering humility
of loving one's own
really loving them
not just conditionally
the good
the bad
the ugly
parts of them
not just the easy parts
even the parts
one nearly hates
about them
the lessor parts
the weaker ones
the self destructive
and broken too
humans capable
of loving humans
even humans that hated
instead of hatred
hunting hatred
finding grace and strength
for loving them too
as a part of their Peoples
learning to see
the bigger picture
of what they'd been through
what leads to

deeply seeded
anger and resentments
to begin with
thus learning therein
to love them still
and once one tries it
challenges their self to
'tis so very hard
to sort true hatred
out from projections
and hearts just made
to be most weary

I loved Europe
in innocence
before I even knew why
having been raised
deeply encultured
to not think of it at all
dream led to
to love it that is
not externally moved to
but it was the dreams too
that led me to
to listen so closely
to what others too
were and weren't saying
before challenging depths

were e'er brought into it
I didn't fear
confronting
the uglier parts
first hand
as personal work
too works
whatever they'd come to be
long before I processed
others doing such things
in their own ways
for their own
but 'twas the hunting of me
and my loving
that led me
to have to see all that
and while the contradictions
make sense
they too grossly don't
not in a world declaring
healing is its best interest
in any degree
of relevant meaning

How I love Europe
more than any
will e'er know now
the very heart and spirit

having been bled so deeply
for loving
bleeding into loving
leaning more into it
on principal
of being bled for loving
even the parts I shouldn't
the parts that would
in no good faith
love me back
which are most likely
such a mess is it
if my life has been
an incidental teacher
but it doesn't matter
'twas America
and the conflicts herein
that made Europe
relevant
in sensing a wholeness
and a more whole becoming
like it too did
for most others
for themselves too

E'er prior
little of that
post peak

Celtic influence
for Europe
would it've
made much sense
but 'twas here
here in America
and nowhere else
could it've been
that I gained
such a lens
of Europe
again perhaps
shattering apart
even Indo relations
in more ways
than most
could fathom

A complex mix
of just the right
ancestry
chemistry
so no one part
could be pulled on
thread like
to be relied upon
and not find itself
woven
with the whole

somehow
illuminating
the tapestry
that I now know
as the North
in me bones
a very old song
that others too
have better tales of
than what they're willing
to be let widely known

If there truly were
violence in silence
then it would extend
in all
directions
would it not
including those
most exalted
in our times
above all others
as incapable of wrongness
which is untrue
in all dimensions
is it not
or has the loss detachment
made humans
that blind now

TRODDEN HEARTS

Be tender
with your heart
but also
guard it fiercely
fore it is from
unlocking within
our own hearts
that all wellsprings
spring forth
into this world

The baiting
for
heartbreaking
disheartening
heart weakening
tendencies
are as multitudinous
and as real
as the sunrises
and sunsets
any have the chances
to witness
day in
day out
cyclically
ongoing

I think the world
world soul
will continue
intentionally
tension laden
to break our hearts
until we learn
that broken
is not broken
and 'tis
our own work
to guard them
fully
and remain ever open
proportionally

Whom
closes their hearts
more directionally
and whom
labors directionally
to ever open theirs
again and again
those are questions
lacking
it feels as though
I should be asking

But opening
doesn't mean
allowing our hearts
to be walked all over
either
does it
is that not more so
sparing others
from confronting
their own challenges

Sometimes
the most loving
things
we can do
are to set
healthy boundaries
and love
from healthy distances
aren't they
we've all
unlearning
to do

THE REALEST LETTING GO

You don't even know
how beautiful you are
they pine to keep you
from seeing you
on purpose
they don't want you to know
what is in you
what is in you
that they are lacking
or maybe more so
perceive they're lacking
but that's not your problem
either
is it

TROUBLED WATERS

My heart feels
for those
who don't remember
the magick in life
who explain it all
away
as defects
of a mind
psychologically
troubled
traumatized
unsound
never the other way
around
how our loss of memory
that we no longer know it
know it
exists
know it exists explicitly
well it's no wonder
wellness
'tis such a mess

COSMIC FRICTION

Wild hearts
see through it
in the end
can feel
can sense
through empathy's fullness
chains moving in
on them
as anything but
freeing

Therein lies
an age old
problem
doesn't it

DEATH'S SPIRIT

Death
stood before me
again and again
threatening me
grabbing for
mine throat
mine eyes
mine good health
any vital
access point
vitality itself
in hand's reach
each time I smiled
as though death
himself
was weakened
when I smile
death as though
God's hand
one of 'em
at least
one might
go as far
so as to say
no less

God's hands

are both
the source
of all suffering
and causation of evil
in the world
but so too
all the beauty
to be beholden
they've each
their own side
in it

I understand now
am simply not repelled
by it
the Old Testament
fear mongering
more than ever
there's an honesty in it

I silently behold
the beauty
by the resiliency
of my own soul alone

But it's our own fault
in the end

then
isn't it
our own sufferings
those of us
who wanted
to remember
why the world
is how it is

The bittersweet
feeling
of all left unsaid

A RAVENNA LAUGH

Grieve not for me
grieve not for any
left behind
I am learning
those left behind
often see
different
or are shown more
than most
it's why they can't
fit in

Just existing
renders many
rule breakers
intolerably so

In that you
were always enough
for me
I saw too
I was enough
for you
it was but world soul
for whom I was judged
to be wrong for
not not enough for

either
ultimately
but far too much
to make some feel
a wee too small
so there's nothing to grieve
at all
is there

LOVE THE SUCK

To truly inhabit
the life
we've been delivered
and the life
we have
made of it
to walk humbly
through our successes
or the rubble of it
to see the smallest
of gifts
as blessings
and the greatest of hurts
as blessings somehow
too
to garner trust
that somehow
life too
does see
is working
for us
with us

I have seen those
on death's bed
who grieved
through hardships

the whole way
with but brief
little periods of reprieve
from darkness
to then cross through
in full presence
and peace
wanting to stay
yes
but also embracing
heart full
the timeliness
that their time
this go around
was spent
and worthwhile

And I have witnessed
those whose lives
were devotedly
light filled
mostly worked out
in their favor
step after step
to lay upon
death's bed
moving towards

gates of crossing over
with trepidation
and insecurities
previously unseen
so certain were they
prior

I am a skeptic
of silent proportions
as to the qualities
of light and dark
as though
inversion layered

AS TITLED: THOSE MADE MAD

If you knew the extent
to which divinity
outside
of all human controls
steered me
into all 'twas endured
you'd probably weep
in ecstasy and sadness
all at once
for all that had to happen
apparently

But the utterances
the utterances I will not make
tasting into mysteries
alas
that 'twere for me
to have found
my blessings
distinct unto me
for dancing
dancing in silence in
not out of obedience
as some silences
can be
but silence
as a divine act

of defiance
against that
which defiles
sacredness
all around us

May you become
as madly blessed
as well

SANCTITY IN SOME SILENCES

I don't much worry
about where I'm seen
or not seen
or even if I'm seen
anymore
I see me
and that matters
most
somehow

Where I am
well,
I open up
a wee more
share a little bit
more
that I may not
not anymore
with others
otherwise
'tis how it's mostly been
but more
intention laden
now
in the random
little moments
the small ones

per usual for me

And where I am not
well,
I just don't
it all makes more sense
now
and why others
do or don't
and I've not the bandwidth
either
to do it different
to give it
much more thought
focus
than it's already taken

I accept life
as it is
before me
in ways
maybe I didn't
before

I know what it's like
to not be seen
in even your more intimate

of relationships
to have thought you were
and to come to find
that you weren't
even when you were
most you

I know that feeling
of that gutting
of that loss
of overnight
being led to grapple
through the whole
of one's worth
something that once came natural
so as to be instinctual
having long been
hard fought for
the true nature of a human
yet not mind groped through
in a literal sense
in this dehumanizing world
to have it torn out
under you
through you
in you too
externally hunted

so as to question
any of one's worth
then in response

To simply stand naked
before the universe
and ask for
and dream for
absolutely nothing

I remapped the whole
of poverty
in mine heart
through the process
and gave away
everything
I had
everything
I'd built a meager
life around
everything
I'd ever known
a deep dive in trusting
more than can be
explained
through any
worded language

I've lost more
than most could handle
more than once now
and I've faith
as in before
life will once more
gift me more
than most
somehow

To feel that
that kind of support
innate
as life wrecks over you
God's hands
no less
to know it as such
at last
well,
there're simply no words
a silence
hard earned
and blessings
the same
no need for words
for any such things

LONG DAYS SHORT YEARS

I could no more go back
as I could not jump forward
a place and mixture of feelings
I have known before
but this was about
God's hands' needs
for witnessing it
not that in me
oh, the triteness

STAGED NDE

Something happens
when death comes
to overtake a soul
while still living
for those that've
lived little
many a soul
become
enlivened
for those that've
lived a plenty
lived vividly
having already known
such things
in their own ways
quietly
when such a death
is forced on them
like a rape
for show
for some need of others
for display
for diplomacy
one could even say
well,
something very different
becomes of them

WILD CARD

I've already lived a life
that most wouldn't understand
so why would I want or need
the next chapter
to be any different

HALLOWED SAVAGERY

Tell them
to take
their beef
made for taking
out of here

I am kinder
than a chickadee
more playful
like a fawn
or foal
for that matter
a touch that can be
more lovingly gentle
than a butterfly's wings
more compassionate
and empathic
than their own mother
likely
until one corners me
cages me
bullying me
gang like
cornered
against silence
against projections
against demands

against love of self
itself

Then
then I am as savage
as this land
I find my self in
at present
perhaps the very reason
I landed
where I did
with so much
of the planet
opened up
as a canvas
before me

PERMEABILITY

If there is anything
that speaking with the ancestors
has most shown me
'tis the line
the very edge
as though a veiled horizon
fingertips in front of me
in which
it melts away
and forms again

THANK YOU

Thank you
for becoming
what you would
not've
wanted

EURO CHURCH GREENHORN

I stared me own demons
down
dead center
broad daylight
no hiding needing
not on my part
not for those parts
of me
I could care less
who saw those sides
of me

And I laughed
and I smiled
about it
so certain were they
I did not know them
like psilocybin
had taught me
nothing
that I was
well experienced
like that
and still me
that
they could not
fathom

let alone
that mycelial wonders
like the sacredness
of water
like all that flows through
may've medicined me
into the me
they perceived
they were witnessing
or believed they were
to begin with

How many saw me
as a contradiction
to love
as anything but
but from mine eyes
that was but
the mirror
they needed to see
just to be able to
cope
with keeping their eyes
ever glancing
in my direction
without honest exchange
without honesty

BUT A WHISPER

How the rains came
rain after rain after rain
a deluge
a flooding
the undamming
of all sacred rivers
and I learned that way
what it was
to walk on water
and the melting
of the ice caps
made so much more sense
why 'twas needful
and how easy 'twould be
to reverse
such simple
human actions
such simple
human concerns
the planet
this biosphere
is as easy to cool
as it is to heat
like water
just like us

PLUVIOPHILE

Divinity is in them
divinity is in you
divinity is in me
why is it
they are only ever
interested
in pointing fingers
out
as to why
it doesn't work
I'm over here
all on me own
seeing the tapestry
in wholeness
everything attached
I can't not see
like that

It was easy this time
to let go
after a few tears shed
a reminder of
how alive I am
even though some think
this
the realm of the dead

GROWING PAINS

I look around
at all the cruelty
in words even
masked as love
in the great conversation
comprising world soul
in those words
most of all
maybe
if ever there was
violence in words
as a form
of unseen violence
terrorism against souls
as I was led
to call it
blatant contradiction world making

Such a turning away
from divinity
being in all
at all times
in all times
that nothing existed
unfolded
in isolation
away from world soul

nothing of recorded
history
at least

A lesson
that in all
hardships
trials
sufferings
world soul
'tis ever present
guiding it
the turning away
therefore
'tis in that denial
in times
of great enlightenment
across world soul
there is a heightened risk
that in those times
most of all
humanity's blind spots
will've grown
will grow to be
more unseeable
and that's sort of how
the world

looks to me
as of recently

A humanity
fighting itself
in all directions
from looking
to see itself
as it is
in all directions

Let their blinds spots
grow
let them swell
to never before seen
proportions
if it must be
let them be
and say
and project
onto you
all they see
you to be

Know my dear
that your blind spots
too

will swell
have swollen
will grow too
as your empathy
has already proven

I am here
to hold you
love you
through it all
to maybe even
love them
distantly
despite their
so sure
infallibility

It's divinity
working
through all of us
ultimately
is it not
so let it be
all it will be
all it must be
I guess

I can confess
oh, it will hurt
to see
as all blind spots do
but so too will theirs
though differently
as theirs are not
the same
as yours

But I assure you
as I saw
am still learning
each step in my journey
yours is a hurt
that will've been
worth
every hurt
and fear
to've seen
I so too
hope
is theirs
ultimately

THINK ABOUT IT

Have you ever given thought
about ancient Greece
I mean the Celts
were chilling there
far bigger than Greece
and it's almost like
they barely existed
like indigenous Europe
never did
outside of Near East
relations with it
like it is ghosted
still
the whole of it now
as though it matters
less than
everywhere else
and not just the Peoples
but the land itself

We know from ancient
mystery schools
and from indigenous
teachings
those formally
recognized
that is

far too many ghosted
in those contexts
designedly
that people were moving
and exchanging
all around the world
so isn't it interesting
how extensive the Celts were
and yet
how little
they're acknowledged
and how few think
it speaks of their roots
and yet to them
it does so strongly
which of course
makes perfect sense
if we truly understood
all that it was
still is

I look back
to those embers
the phoenix
burning
on the floor
and I can't help
but wonder
what it was
I saw
forget what others thought
they saw

'Twas the first time
I had to consciously
and silently hold
piercing eyes
in all directions
projection laden
ridiculing
with but only a few
love filled
and yet
to receive so much love
still
more love almost
than I could handle
and to know

beyond all knowing
that all that love
mattered more
and carry on then
as though 'twas nothing
at all
with many eyes
demanding
I see me self
as what they saw
another pathetic
little
blond haired
blue eyed
white girl
for having experienced
anything
as though we don't

The shame
the shame they were hoping
I would carry
in that I didn't
only angered them
more
and I had no choice
but to let them

carry instead
their own baggage
baggage made seen
in projections
they needed
in that moment

How heavy
I saw them then
and how lightened
was my spirit
despite the overwhelm
lightened by something
far beyond me

But the death
the death that followed
and the trembling too
that said everything
unsaid
didn't it
that I was not
that out of touch
that something
indeed
real
had transpired

that I was
more loved
than one human
could ever know
and what was experienced
as hate
was but for
what others saw
in my eyes
and reflected little
of my soul

I wish we all
felt that
innately
that none had to
demand that
be filled externally
of the world
for them
the exaltations
and debasements
the roots of all dehumanization

I know there was
a time
when we used to

oh, how corrupted
humanity
has become
to insist
the feeding into
constant
insatiable vacuums

It begs the question
does world soul
even know
how to create
anything different

HEART SHAPED LEAVES

Of star, bird, and plant
water, wind, and stone
animal and soil
dust is particle
I heard that song
a very old one
as sweet as
the hymns
of a red-winged
black bird
or a lark
to be more honest
sweeter still
like pan himself
or her
named differently
a mirror of each
in each
mirroring
one another
what flows between
calling me
like the oldest of callings
back into me
and you
back into you
if you'd heard it

Then what of God's
mirrored
counterpart
I am led to ask
is it that different
why has
world soul
as though God
himself
why does
world soul
keep him from her
again and again
in the stories
from islands
to mainlands
small nations
to what would become
empires
that it does not matter
it patterns over
like keeping the feminine
out of God
as though God is not
in everything
what is so fearful
in such love

is it God that fears
unconditional loving

Hearts
positioned
for upholding
denying heart
like the damning
of rivers free flowing
salmon cut off
from following
the sweet scents
of their beloved
home streams
as sweet
and as permeating
as a lilac grove
intoxicating
nearly
so strong
one must
learn their own
grounding
in it
to stay centered
in their own
heart and soul

or the whole
of the movement
shakes
against them
doesn't it

To be so alive
with life
what many want
to call death
well,
'tis no wonder
the world's being
made to be
as it is

Is it death
or is it life
is it heaven
or is it hell
a dark age
or a golden one

Does it really matter
what we call it
isn't that part
of the problem

MATTER SAMPLING

In our most truthful
moments
it doesn't matter much
what others think
about us
if they think of us
at all
odds are
they don't

I look outwardly
these days
mostly
to be inspired
and
to witness
pulsations
of world soul
in intuited moments
flow channels
to have some
cognition
of relational synergies
and how they are moving
in our ever weaving
present
but that's about it
all I care to handle

KNOW YOUR WHY

I watch her grow
before me eyes
her eyes
full of surprise
limitlessly
of all the things
I feel good about
it's about being
her mother
knowing
that my greatest
responsibility
to her
is to teach her
to listen inward
to teach her
to live
to live well
no matter
the externally
swirling
circumstances
and above all else
to live unmediated
with a resilient heart
here for all of it

TRANSMUTATION IS WORK
OF THE PERSONAL

When you understand
the enormity
of world soul
that globalization
is
world soul's creation
with all its violence
in spreading
and maintaining
the sum of it
all of it
you'd stop pointing fingers
and hunt the anger
about it
within
again and again
no matter one's direction
or positioning

You'd learn to let go
to let go of all of it
and be your own savior
the light of Christ
wasn't meant
to only be seen
outside of us

we are that
and so much more
even in the simplest
of lifes
like finding joy
in the simplest
of moments
it's not that different

ALL IN ALL

The sun
had waged war
on me
until I became dreamless
learning that importance
its own gift
but 'twas the moon again
the moon
who secretly
gifted me space
unseen
to dream
again
as me
the moon and all the sun eclipses
yet the moon alone
mirroring
the moon in me
'tis the moon in me
who loves
loves freely

LET THE WINDS CARRY WEIGHT AWAY

When we slowly
move into
grace and presence
not fixed and finished
done or not done
but e'er a work
in progress
for some of our more
cycle breaking
blind spots
to clarify
like purifying
tainted water
sullied
by time's illusions
and we all have 'em
our own distinct lenses
are we each
in this world
so too
in doing so
does it become
more accessible
to us
to then witness
blind spots
of world soul

mirrored
somehow
and gravity too then
gravity
as troubles
and terribleness
lightens too
somehow

SELF REFLECTION

I looked in the mirror
one day
and realized
in slow and steady pause
I was already
the woman
I wanted to be
a woman that could survive
anything
that did not literally
kill me
that I could still
laugh
and smile
in the face
of any of it
no matter who
or what
had delivered it
that there would never
not be
magick on my path
every step of the way
guiding me
that everything
I truly needed
would find its way

into my life
or prove to me
I didn't need it
that I didn't have to
buy
into
any illusions
even the so sure
visions
of the collective
world soul

That freedom
dwells
in the spirit
and the heart
most of all

DAM REMOVAL

Your thirst
your hunger
cannot be filled
by elevating
and seeking
in others
what it is
you seek

Idolizing
the ways
of another
of others
any others
is often
more delusional
and therefore
light years
more dangerous
for both
you and any them
than confronting
deceptions
within
from pursuing
all needed
within

To tap into
our own timelessness
is ever
at
any of our fingertips
trust none
that say different
that you need them
or another
to tune into it
the tales of Knockgrafton
once warned
of such risks

THE SPRINGS OF LIFE

Your heart
'tis yours alone
'tis none others
even if before another
we open it
dare lay it down
dare to think we need to
to be loved at all

It is still ours
still beats for us
still pumps our blood
still feeds our lungs
the very powerhouse
for all that flows
through any of us

None other can take it
from any other
regardless
of how any
may want to
so guard your heart
fiercely
as though it may be
the most important work
you do

because it may be

Guarding one's heart
may be
the most sacred of intelligence
of all

A FOUNTAIN OF FORGIVENESS

Through you
no one else but you
through you
all is forgivable
and they may hate you
for that
misunderstand you
greater still
that you have such
grace and strength
humility and grounding
simply put
the resiliency
to live that
and smile more
but you do so
and more
quite wondrously so
'tis no wonder
they project
so much
on your shoulders
or pretend to
at least
they're hoping
it'll stick somehow

and yet
but by God's grace
it doesn't
does it

THE OVERCOMING

He taught me
to see through
human ignorance
and belly roll
laugh within it
about it
at all of it
in all directions
but he still had a way
of holding space for it
in ways that matched
me own heart's
better movements
and in doing so
he helped me to grow
through it
until a hold on me
it no longer held

STRANGE ESTRANGEMENTS

I love the feeling
of being
in an ecology
unfamiliar to me
out of my element

Don't get me wrong
I love the intimacy
of fully being
at ease
knowing the communities
plants
animals
mycology
how the soils came to be
the very way water
moves through a landscape
the energies
for better and worse
a place
gives rise to
or those that it swallows
but there's a wonder
to it
feeling slightly alien
and a glee then too
in seeing friendly faces

without really knowing
much else beyond
them

The excitement
the trepidation
the curiosity
the methodical hesitations
the need to pay
exceedingly
close attention
to see many details
one can be certain
even most locals
neglect the time
to take in
these days

The wild
has taught me
that
unmediatingly
how few see it
at all
how landscapes
miss humans
seeing them at all

most indigenous
not even tuned in
these days
not anymore
not any more or less
than many are

THE ARDUOUS MOLT

You've changed me
my, have you changed me
the sensuous dance
when one's eyes
as beholder
are changed
like a forever altered
skyline
different
but the same
a surfing
of finding
waves of continuity
instead of
a fracturing
away
was everything gained
not worth precision
of what 'twas required
to see it

WORTH MORE THAN GOLD

I lost near everything
and yet somehow
I gained the world
in my own small way
and opening
entirely unchained
despite tears of grief
for broken dreams
for a dissolution
of all I'd ever known
or been
seemingly
but the deepened
awakening
to the timeless
elements
that rounded out
those already shown
known
through lived experiences
alone
a priceless
exchange

PEACE BECAME ME

The chords
the chords so out of key
with applied
applications
of awakening
group making
to be inconvenient
is to not fit
not fit into
the accustomed harmonies
fore stolen are some
or turned fashionable
as an after effect
auto-tuned
somehow

Everyone wants
a new song
of sorts
somehow
someway
without changing the tune
the very frequencing
of drumming
drumming as heart beats
the striking of keys
lungs breathing

informal music making
made more beautiful
the glorious lure
of new sound
unfamiliar
yet timelessly resonant
and deeply familiar
therefore

The measure
of being at peace
without change
in conditions
for how the world is
exists
at present
'tis little else
like it

A TRILLION FRACTAL SUN

The wild
that there is wild still
is not
what most think
it to be
nor are those
who stand for it
on any side making
we're not that different
really
though different
very much
we also are
somehow
so I've learned
in the hardest of ways

It's more in our stories
isn't it
and our blind spots
too
our acceptances of
and denials of
reality
and world making
how much more permeable
it all is

but then too
how that permeability
folds back in
on itself
like time collapsing
in divine presence
of all that made
all of it
and the timelessness
of sacredness then
in matter
like galaxy clusters
aligning
painting
the whole of the night sky
far grander
than the milky way
and how tales
of permeability
then too mislead
and mislead rather deeply
as though trying to collapse
sacredness itself
into a black hole
away from creation
a cosmic impossibility
yet again though
isn't it

INFINITE EMPHEMERAL FRIENDS

Hawks circle me
doves swarm me
as though blessing me
or cueing me into
that I am blessed
with feathers dropping
like a smudging or dusting
of the air around me
songbirds sing with me
lure me to sing with them
while corvids coo me
one time
for o'er an hour on end
I gift them gifts sometimes
they are like friends

Butterflies savor nectar
from salt on my skin
mayflies too
my favorite
of aquatic bugs
do you even ponder
aquatic bugs
do you know their importance
have you ever stood before
a hatch swirling you
and laughed in ecstasy

at how beautiful it was
would it even
make you smile

I saw a raven last week
up close
looked more like
a golden eagle
unlike any seen before
eagle or raven
so routinely
do I see things
that defy
known possibilities
I can't not be
mesmerized
and carried through
feeling loved and supported
even if 'tis an illusion
when examined
from a world soul
perspective
looking at degrees
of human connection
but there's more to life
than that
isn't there

Perhaps I am an alien
after all
or maybe world soul is
world soul as alien
to nature
blind spotted
by the collective
denial
of all that is
and isn't possible
too

CONTENTMENT

When you realize
your life
will never not have
meaning
'tis a wondrous
feeling
to see so clearly
just existing
is enough
for thine own self
'tis a richness
a richness that cannot be
faked
nor taken

LIFE IS NOT BROKEN

I walk these woods
now
ne'er the same
again
could they be
but 'tis okay
too
though e'er does me heart
ache a little
walking them
for the songs
they sing
before us
all said and unsaid
in the chorus
a chorus so grand
no banner of heaven
could silence
the glory of it

I walk these woods
more alone
than ever
yet never alone
still

I want to walk woods

even more gutted
more fragmented
and less loved
fringes holding on
to love them more
fully
to whisper back
reverberate
in the old ways
at all that would witness me
I see them
still
and they are
just as beautiful
as ever
to watch then
how they'd flourish
after

OUR ORBIT

The trinity
the round dance
all the ways
I was tested
to see
if I would move
towards
or away from
against
or in grace with
you
where would my heart
be led
authentically lead me
to

I could focus
on a them
in regards to that
determined
to keep me
from you
but what good
would that bring
when laws of attraction
are brought into it

My gaze
now ever refining
having learned
from experiential
witnessing
love deceiving
from love timeless
love taking
from love giving
reciprocation
not baiting
but love making
our art
in living

'Tis no wonder
they hate it
but no longer either
do we have to grow
resentments
for what is in us
aimed to be
externally
denied unto us
'tis all a choice
a countervailing
now

and the tides
the tides of the world
are being made
for each
to be
what they are

Sit with you
hear you
hold you
dance with you
these I will do
perhaps even before
you even see me
see me embracing
you

I was never one
to submit
never good at
much even softening
feeling so intimately
all the hostilities
in motion
in the greater world
but in dancing
with you

surrendering
I do
with you
surrender
before the sacredness
of all of life
and it's simply
wonderful
to let me guard go
even if
not a soul
but me own
ever notices

THE FORBIDDEN LABYRINTH

Misconstrued
are notions of shapeshifting
in near all multitudes
of dimensions
lost in translations
so many meanings
layers within layers
the least of which
'tis humility
through the body
experience
that is not yours

You learn to see
through the eyes
to better understand
how another
thinks
feels
experiences
the more skilled
in shapeshifting
the better the understanding
potential

What happens
if one does not return

fully to their body
though
what happens
in fields of empathy
when we listen
too closely
and forget how much
we too matter
being grounded in it
is the loss detachment
really that different

And what of what happens
when not all shapeshift
what happens
when not all hold
much any compassion
for you
surviving it
all worth asking
before we even get to
being worthy too
of thriving

BE BRAVE LIKE JACK HE WHISPERED BACK

I look across the pages
of my ancestral becoming's
and so much of its mythos
'tis detailed
for capturing
its own boxing in moments
by globalization
portrayed through love
and love being denied
to love
unashamedly
love itself
by foreign and domestic
demands
in attempts
to forge a new world
as though lacking
sun and moon
itself
constructed light making
for controlling
the whole of the world
nay
the whole of the cosmos
from a one centered
not galactic center
place

So I learned to breathe
underwater
from the mermaids
and the mermaids
they taught me well
gladly did they
before I knew
what that meant
to me
remythologizing
is not a metaphor

And time folded
back in
on itself
and I was in
all time
again
in the present moment

The danger
in our attention
wherever
we give it
is learning
to see
to sense

sixth sensed like
sometimes
collectors
sometimes
collectors
who know not
what they do
but their words
still confess to it
in subtleties
listen ever closely

Follow always
the goodness
of your own heart
it already knows
where you are meant
to move towards

THE GIANT OF ALL GIANTS

I come from many
stolen from Europe
never bought and paid for
like those sold abroad
by their own
a debt that has yet
to be confronted
by world soul

Everyone thinks
academia
holds the keys
to our pasts
failing
in all assumptions
so overly trusting
to richly grasp
the one dimensional
notion
of such a nature
no matter who
it inserts
in there
like forgetting everything
one must learn
in a foundational
statistics class

So long as it is bound
to power
curiosity
loses ground
to power players
a long line
of easily corruptible humans
is never in short supply
and fewer and fewer
questions are asked
how history
is always written
by the victors
those who garnered power
in chapters
not simply those
who survived power
allowed to be recounted
as they came to be

For anyone being
more honest in that
our histories too
those of the common folk
me and you likely
worked into the ground
to be buried at best

while still breathing
are not to be found
in any such pages
but rather in the stories
of simpletons
grains in folk songs
and poetic trails
countless steps
no prose and parvenu
represent us
but artistic expressions
and all that comes through
creative
actions and works
most burned
in tiny corners
or locked up
in dark closets
under the pedigrees
in formalized archiving
to remain
unconsidered
as though preserved
for little more purpose
than saying
'twas done
that it captured them too

The peoples' stories
the people's stories
are never in the politics
of it
or what's politically
relayed
about it
not unlike today
the politics of it
never or rarely
represent the people
just as the stories
made
too rarely don't
not in a merchant class
ordering
of the world
lobbyists
have the highest powers
as they have
all the way back
to late stage Rome
and earlier
elsewhere
likely

But that's changing

isn't it
those dynamics
holding such power
there is an opening
at least
for it to change
only time will tell
though
because that's been intended
before too
far more than once

The bigger question
remains
will we learn from history
will world soul
itself
in its gargantuan
enormity
all powerful
over everyone
have the courage
to read more closely
have the courage
to witness
its own blind spots
now that's an interesting

question
isn't it
and a rather
unpopular one
mind you

BUT A FLIGHT AWAY

Time was never
going to take me far
take any of us far
from that which we love
only is there
the illusion
that it does

CARTWHEEL DISPLAY

I wanted freedom
like the eagle's wings
like what he gifted me
more appropriately
what he showed me
'twas always
my birthright
was always in me

But how does one
teach another
to fly
in trying times
other than holding
them down
as though talons locked
in an aerial
down spiraling
flight
towards the ground
until they realize
they are anything but
broken
the trust it takes
to do so together
a bond that changes
both forever

AEIOU
2
but for very different
reasons likely
helping me sort out
my own insanities
with absolute brevity
in a mad
mad world
without needing
heaven
nor heaven's entry

AN OLDER VINTAGING

My heart belongs
with not to
those whose hearts
are so open
yet rightly guarded
that they've the strength
and resiliency
to humanize
just about any human
by mere choice
of their own choosing
not because
any other(s)
say
they can or can't
must or shan't
nor does their inner compass
listen to such dogmas
no,
not the tepidly
excitable
fumbling
fickle
untrustable
love
that all directional hearts
in America

so often exude
all I've seen
and been bullied and bruised
by
as love prior
and far more
than me
this land of savagery
Covid proven
for all eyes to see
and every crisis
previously
truly
love built
entirely around
conditional agreement
explicitly
banner waving
in excessive surety
they interest me little

But the former
the former
so few even see
their own self's as such
likely
worked into corners

life led them to choose
but witnessing them
they taught me
they showed me
who I was
by loving
how my heart loves

What it means
to be wild hearted
without ever knowing
or seeing me
synchronicity alone
led me to see them
as they are
though most'd disagree likely
what they gifted me
'tis for me
to've seen
regardless
that's how my trusting
works in it

TIMELESS BEAUTY

Do you see
how you light
other's aglow
even those
who turn
and take it out
on you
it's not the whole truth

Freedom
'tis a costly thing
that you see all this
and lift them up
still
you are a giant
of hearts
and yet
you walk as small
as any (hu)man

You are perfectly you
perfectly European
perfectly all that came before
all the aforementioned
and thus too
all that will outlast
such definitioning's

if you want to
whether in this world
or the next

THE INVISIBLE HAND

From Australia
to South Africa
to the Wildest West
of America
the Americas
there's an untold
remembrance
rememberers
in living memory
of all that led
to there

Little of what
this society
tells us it to be
entitlements
ya mean worthy
of surviving it
worthy of not being
buried still

Somewhere between
here and there
place and time
not that different
than we find
in our present

movement of
bodies
goods
diseases
energies
Empire
who was really
moving it

UNCASTING THE RUBICON

I became the wind
that day
the very air
that those winds
carry
I felt freedom's
return
the lightness
of it
I felt how light
pierces
through me
like divine sun rays
God beams
some call 'em
but never in me
had I felt them
before that day
nor ne'er prior
did I see them
in others
not really
not as such
before that day

UNORTHODOX BIRTH

There is nothing like
birthing a soul
into the world
to teach you
about the delicate
balance
between
life and death
being alone
and entirely unalone

Made it to 9cm
with little more support
than an occasional
breathing
ever so lightly
upon mine neck
no one could help me
but me
through all that

I'd never been there
before
I was just doing
what my body
and soul
knew to do

'twas my mind alone
that questioned my self
if I had it in me

I didn't realize
how far I'd made it
all on my own
until it came time
thinking I had
a much longer marathon
ahead of me
than what was reality
the best news of my life
fore I knew in that moment
I had it in me
and more

She felt bad
for having not been there
but my body
didn't follow
any of the rules
go figure
so none of us knew

When it came time
for pushing

then
I wasn't alone
inside
or
outside
that surrendering
that moment
determinate between
my own ring of fire
and the back cracking
pressure
coming through me
no drugs
not one
to rely on
to ease it
didn't even want one
not even in that moment
not once I knew
where I'd made it to

I wanted to
experience
all of it
I wanted to know
my strength
I wanted to know

the strength
of all women
that'd come
before me
and that surrendering
that surrendering
there is nothing else
quite like it

IN GOOD FAITH

When you cross
that threshold
where God
as universe too
is before you
and the card is in
God's hand
one of 'em even
to demonstrate
reciprocal faith
in your tried
and tested
proven faith

Where you are
one
with all of it
all of the elements
harmonized
as you inside
in a world
in a world so far removed
from remembering it
as such
there 'tis not even a word
for that freedom
is there

nor the temptuous pulls
to take one
out of it

May the rivers
of life
be so unleashed
within you
that you become
the joy
the love
the alchemical blessing
of your own life

ACKNOWLEDGEMENTS

As it began, so too it ends. Grateful for all of it.

www.ingramcontent.com/pod-product-compliance
Lightning Source LLC
Chambersburg PA
CBHW031307160726
47993CB00001B/325